A Book About Red Pandas
AMAZING EARTH: Wild Animal Facts
Written and designed by Dawon Seashore

Dawon Seashore

A Book About About Red Pandas

FOR KIDS

Dear reader,

We are happy to present to you **A Book About Red Pandas**. This book is part of our Wild Animal Facts series where we take a look at some **amazing facts** about Earth's many fascinating animals.

The book was created for all youngsters out there, and any curious adult, who love to learn more about their favorite creatures.

We sincerely hope you enjoy and have fun reading. After, you can find out if you learned something new in a **fun quiz** at the end of the book. There are lots of beautiful photos as well!

Be sure to leave a **review** to let us know how you liked the book. It helps a lot to improve and expand on future publications.

Sincerely yours,

Wild Animal facts Team

TABLE OF CONTENT

SCIENTIFIC NAME: *Ailurus fulgens* (Ailurus comes from the ancient Greek word *ailouros* which means "cat")

The red panda has many nicknames: firefox, lesser panda, and red-cat-bear. But what is a red panda really?

Is it a cat?

A bear?

Or maybe a racoon?

READ ON TO FIND OUT!

WHAT ARE THEY?

First of all, red pandas are mammals* which means they have fur and feed their young with milk.

We all know the lovable bamboo-eating white and black giant pandas native to Asia's high forests.

Even though these pandas and the red panda are in some ways similar and share a name,

Giant panda

Red panda

the two are NOT closely related.

*if the words in yellow are a bit hard for you to understand, look up what they mean in the glossary at page 41-42

Red pandas are much smaller than giant pandas.

Red panda   **Giant panda**

Giant pandas are part of the bear family.

Red pandas were first thought to be part of the raccoon family because of their similar physical traits.

Later, they were put into the bear family (where giant pandas are).

Now, red pandas are placed in their own unique family—the Ailuridae.

Did you know?

Red pandas are the only living member of the family Ailuridae!

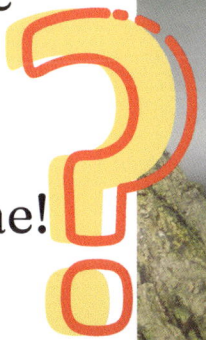

HOW BIG ARE THEY?

14.6 – 18.6 in

22 – 24.6 in

Adult red pandas are larger than a house cat.

They typically weigh between 8 and 17 pounds (3.6 and 7.7 kilograms).

They are 22 to 24.6 inches (56 to 62.5 centimeters) long. Their tail adds another 14.6 to 18.6 inches (37 to 47.2 centimeters) to their lenght.

WHAT DO THEY LOOK LIKE?

You can recognize a red panda by its reddish-brown coat.

Its belly and legs are black as well as the tip of its tail.

Long, bushy tail helps keep balance and protects red pandas from harsh cold and winds.

Thick fur completely covers their feet which have five, separated toes. They even have fur on their paws!

Their claws are sharp and can be pulled back like a cat.

13

It has small triangle-shaped ears.

It has long whiskers around the mouth and chin.

Did you know?

Like giant pandas, red pandas have a false "thumb" to help them eat bamboo and climb trees. It is not a real finger because it comes from a small bone within the wrist of the panda's paw.

WHERE DO THEY LIVE?

HABITAT – Red pandas mostly live in **temperate forests** with bamboo in the Himalayas and other high mountains from northern Myanmar (Burma) to southwest China. They can also be found in Nepal, India and Tibet.

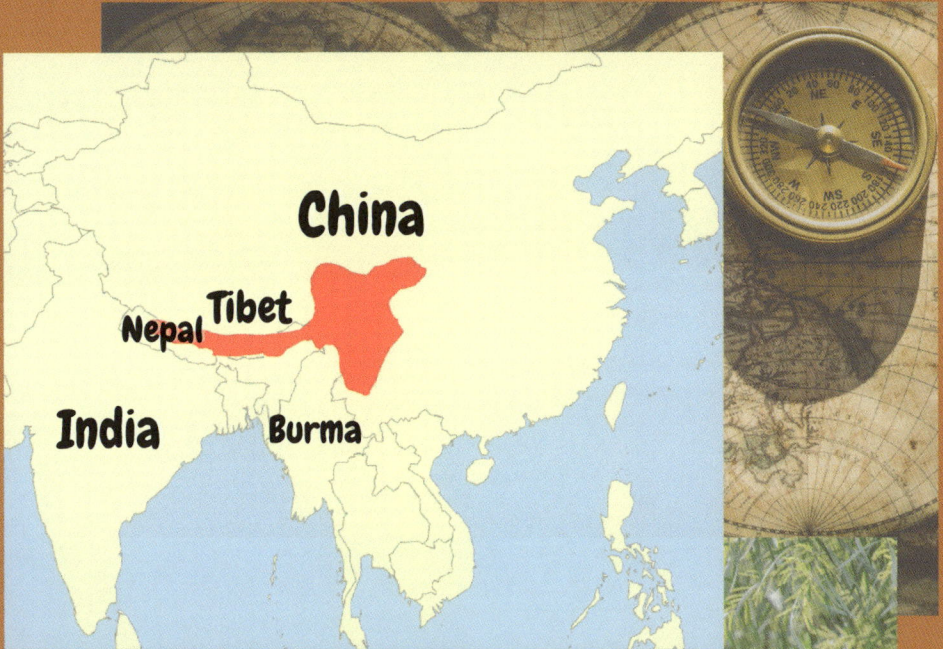

WHAT DO THEY EAT?

Red panadas are mostly herbivores.
Bamboo makes up about 95% of their diet.

They also search for roots, acorns, fruits, insects, and occasionally they eat birds and small mammals.

Did you know?

Red pandas eat A LOT of bamboo. They can digest only about 24 percent of the bamboo they eat so they need to eat about 2 to 4 pounds (1 to 2 kilograms) of bamboo leaves each day. That's 20 to 30 percent of their body weight!

COMMUNICATION

Red pandas are generally shy and quiet but can communicate with each other when in danger.

They stand on their back legs and may use their sharp paws when they feel stressed or in danger. Remember to keep your distance if you see a standing red panda!

Red pandas are skilled climbers. They use trees for shelter, to escape **predators** and to sunbathe in the winter.

A red panda typically rests or sleeps in trees or other high places so it is difficult to observe in the wild.

It lies down on branches with legs hanging when it is HOT,

and it curls up with its tail over its face when it is COLD.

DAILY LIFE

Red pandas are mostly active at night as well as dawn and dusk.

DAWN - the first daylight that appears in the morning

DUSK- the time of day just before night

On average, they are awake half of the day while the rest of the time they spend resting or sleeping in trees.

They are more active in cooler weather, especially during the winter mating season.

FAMILY LIFE

Red pandas are shy except when mating.

Mating occurs mostly between January and March.

Mother red pandas make a nest in tree holes, tree roots or between bamboo trees. They cover the nest with leaves, moss and other soft plant material.

Red pandas grow in their mother for three months.

Mothers give birth usually between May and August.

Newborn cubs are covered in thick grey fur and their eyes and ears are closed.

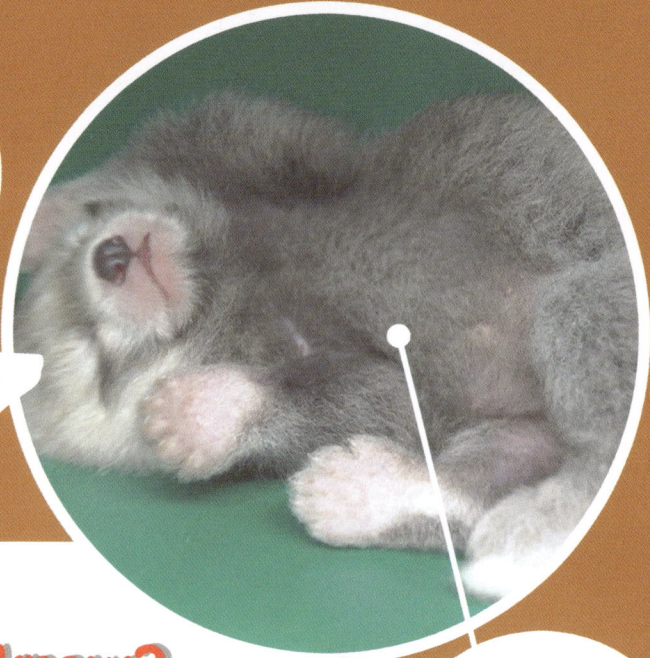

Eyes and ears are closed.

Did you know?

Red pandas are born completely covered in fur to protect them from the cold environment!

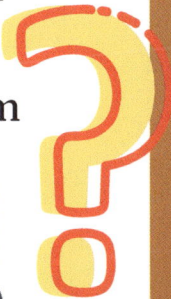

Body is completely covered in grey fur.

Photo by Nicole Nicassio-Hiskey, courtesy of the Oregon Zoo.

29

Cubs usually come in twos, but a litter can be anywhere from one to four siblings.

Young red pandas stay with their mother until they are full-grown which is about one year.

Red pandas are ready to mate at around 18 months of age.

INTERESTING FACTS

1

Red pandas have <u>extremely flexible ankles</u> which makes it possible for them to climb headfirst down tree trunks.

ANKLE- flexible part of the leg just above the foor

They are one of the few animals on the planet that can do that!

2

The white on their face is well visible in the dark. It can help guide a mother's lost cub in the darkness!

Red on their backs is the same color as the moss on the trees where they live.

Their red and black fur color is camouflage to hide red pandas from their predators.

Black fur on their stomach makes it hard to see them up in the trees from the ground.

When it gets really cold, red pandas go into what is called torpor. They wrap their fluffy long tail around themselves and go into a deep sleep, lowering their body temperature and slowing down their breathing. This way they save their energy.

LIFESPAN

In the wild, red pandas live 8 years on average.

In captivity, they can live to about 14–15 years.

Did you know?

Red pandas may live as long as 23 years!

Female red pandas do not have cubs after age 12, while males continue to make offspring.

FUTURE OF RED PANDAS

STATUS: endangered

There are **less than 10,000** red pandas in the whole world!

Red pandas are victims of deforestation. Forests are destroyed so they lose their home. Also, there is less bamboo to eat. That's why the population of red pandas is smaller and smaller each year.

QUIZ TIME!

1. Red pandas are part of what family?
a) bear
b) raccoon
c) cat
d) its own unique family

2. What does a red panda mostly eat?
a) fish
b) insects
c) bamboo
d) other animals

3. How many fingers does a red panda have?
a) three
b) four
c) five
d) six

4. How long do mother red pandas carry their babies?
a) three months
b) four months
c) six months
d) nine months

5. What color is a red panda's belly?
a) red
b) black
c) white
d) brown

6. Where do red pandas live?
a) in hot deserts
b) in the ocean
c) in temperate forests
d) in the jungle

7. How are red pandas born?
a) without fur
b) with a little bit of fur
c) with fur on their bellies
d) completely covered in fur

8. When are red pandas mostly active?
a) in spring
b) in summer
c) in autumn
d) in winter

9. How many red pandas are there in the world?
a) 1 million
b) 500 000
c) 10 000
d) less than 10 000

Bonus question: ?

10. What helps red pandas climb down trees headfirst?
a) flexible ankles
b) sharp claws
c) long legs
d) an extra thumb

Did you finish the quiz? Well done!

Don't worry if you didn't know the answer to all of the questions at first.

You can go back and read through the book again to find the missing answers.

Hopefully you had fun reading and learned some new amazing facts about your favourite animal.

P.S.
Just in case you didn't manage to find all the answers in the end, we put them here for you to look up.
ANSWERS: 1.d), 2.c), 3.c), 4.a), 5.b), 6.c), 7.d), 8.d), 9.d), 10.a)

GLOSSARY

camouflage: a way of hiding something by covering or coloring it so that it looks like its surroundings

cubs: young of some mammals, such as the bear, lion, and wolf

deforestation: the process of cutting down the trees of a forest

endangered: in danger of becoming extinct. When an animal is endangered, it means that few of those animals exist now, and it is possible that there will be no more of them in the future

habitat: the natural environment of an animal or plant

herbivore: type of animal that mostly eats plants

in captivity: animals that are held by humans and prevented from escaping, for example, in a shelter or zoo

in the wild: animals living free in nature

mammals: animals that have fur and feed their young with milk

mating: a male and female of the same animal coming together to make baby animals

mating season: time of year when a type of animal makes babies

native: an animal or plant found naturally in some place

observe: to watch something in a way that you can learn more about it

offspring: the child or young of a human, animal, or plant

population: the number of the same animal living together in the same place

predator: an animal that hunts other animals for food

scientific name (of an animal): a name given to an animal by scientists when they find it in nature for the first time

temperate forest: forest in a place where there are four seasons

torpor: when an animal slows down its body processes to save energy, usually when there is less food around

traits: things that make an animal different from other animals

Congratulations!

You have come to the end of this book.

Thank you for reading this far. Here is an extra photo just for you!

Leave us a review on Amazon if you liked the book! ♥

Printed in Great Britain
by Amazon

58055658R00025